VERBS AND ADVERBS

often

actively

love

firmly

soon

run

act

Samantha Green

E | **Enslow Publishing**
101 W. 23rd Street
Suite 240
New York, NY 10011
USA

enslow.com

T0019786

Words to Know

adjective A word used to describe a person, place, or thing.

linking verbs Verbs that connect what a sentence is about with a word that gives information about that thing.

modal verbs Verbs used to show if something is possible, is allowed, or has to be done.

nouns Words that name people, places, or things.

subject The person, place, or thing performing an action in a sentence.

tense The form of a verb that shows when an action took place.

Contents

Loves is also a verb. "Johnny loves ballet."

4

What Is a Verb?

A verb is a word that tells us what is happening. It is the action of a sentence. "Johnny dances ballet." *Dances* is a verb.

FAST FACT

Every complete sentence needs to have a verb.

"Sasha ran on the beach."
Sasha is the noun, and
ran is the verb.

Action Verbs

Action verbs describe what the **nouns** in a sentence are doing. Verbs can tell us if someone walks or runs!

Modal verbs can give us information.
"If the dog eats chocolate, he will get sick."

Modal Verbs

Some sentences also have **modal verbs**. These verbs tell us if something can, will, or must happen. "The dog should eat his own food." Here, *should* is a modal verb.

FAST FACT

Modal verbs are used when asking for permission: "Can I go to the library?"

We use *is* only when talking about one person or one thing, like "the baby."

Linking Verbs

Linking verbs connect the **subject** of a sentence with more information about the subject. "The baby is tired." *Is* links the baby to the feeling *tired*.

FAST FACT

Verbs like *look* can be both action verbs and linking verbs.

Past, present, and future are the three main verb tenses.

Verb Tenses

Verbs also tell us about the timing of an action. We can learn if something happened in the past, is happening now, or will happen in the future.

FAST FACT

Tenses tell the reader if something happened in the past, present, or future.

Some sentences have more than one adverb.

14

What Is an Adverb?

An adverb describes a verb, an **adjective**, or another adverb. "The squirrel quickly climbs the tree." *Quickly* describes how the squirrel climbs.

FAST FACT

Words that end in *-ly* are usually adverbs.

We use the adverb *very* to make the adjective *tasty* more powerful.

16

"How" Adverbs

Adverbs can also answer
questions that ask how.
"The cookie was very tasty."
How tasty was the cookie? *Very*!

Usually, **normally**, and *regularly*
are also "how often" adverbs.

"How Often" Adverbs

Adverbs tell us how often something happens. Does the action happen sometimes, always, or never? "My mom always bakes cookies on Friday." *Always* is an adverb.

"It rained here yesterday."
Here tells us where it rained.

20

On movie sets, "Lights, camera, action" tells people to start filming.

Lights
Camera
Action

"When" and "Where" Adverbs

Adverbs can also show us when and where an action takes place. "It rained yesterday." *Yesterday* describes when it rained.

FAST FACT

When and where adverbs go after the verb or at the end of the sentence.

Learn More

Books

Cook, Julia. *It's Hard to Be a Verb!* Chattanooga, TN: National Center for Youth Issues, 2008.

Heinrichs, Ann. *Adverbs.* Mankato, MN: The Child's World, 2017.

Walton, Rick. *Suddenly Alligator: Adventures in Adverbs.* Layton, UT: Gibbs Smith, 2011.

Websites

ABCYa.com – Nouns and Verbs
http://www.abcya.com/nouns_and_verbs.htm
Play a fun, ice cream–filled game as you learn more about nouns and verbs.

Room Recess – Kid Heroes Verbs
http://www.roomrecess.com/mobile/KidHeroesVerbs/play.html
Pick the right verbs and tenses to be a hero and protect the king!

Index

Published in 2020 by Enslow Publishing, LLC.
101 W. 23rd Street, Suite 240, New York, NY 10011

Copyright © 2020 by Enslow Publishing, LLC

All rights reserved.

No part of this book may be reproduced by any means without the written permission of the publisher.

Library of Congress Cataloging-in-Publication Data

Names: Green, Samantha, author.
Title: Verbs and adverbs / Samantha Green.
Description: New York, NY : Enslow, 2020. | Series: Fun with grammar | Includes bibliographical references and index. | Audience: Grades 1–4. Identifiers: LCCN 2019013639 | ISBN 9781978512795 (library bound) | ISBN 9781978512771 (pbk.) | ISBN 9781978512788 (6 pack) Subjects: LCSH: Grammar, Comparative and general—Verb—Juvenile literature. | Grammar, Comparative and general—Adverb—Juvenile literature. Classification: LCC P281 .G69 2019 | DDC 415/.6—dc23 LC record available at https://lccn.loc.gov/2019013639

Printed in the United States of America

To Our Readers: We have done our best to make sure all websites in this book were active and appropriate when we went to press. However, the author and the publisher have no control over and assume no liability for the material available on those websites or on any websites they may link to. Any comments or suggestions can be sent by email to customerservice@enslow.com.

Photo Credits: Cover, p. 1 Prostock-studio/Shutterstock.com; cover, p. 1 (pencil) OrangeVector/Shutterstock.com; p. 4 vgajic/E+/Getty Images; p. 6 Serega K Photo and Video/Shutterstock.com; p. 8 Monkey Business Images/Shutterstock.com; p. 10 © iStockphoto.com/Oleksandra Troian; p. 12 McCarony/Shutterstock.com; p. 14 shaftinaction/Shutterstock.com; p. 16 Kamira/Shutterstock.com; p. 18 Werner Heiber/Shutterstock.com; p. 20 Coy_Creek/Shutterstock.com; p. 22 AboutLife/Shutterstock.com; interior pages (notebook) Fascinadora/Shutterstock.com; interior pages (pencil) spacezerocom/Shutterstock.com.

Powerful Verbs and Adverbs

Verbs and adverbs fill our world with action! They bring sentences together so we understand what is happening and how it is happening.